My Holy Week Journal

SAINT **SHENOUDA**PRESS

My Holy Week Journal

Designed by

CAROLEEN AKLADIOUS

ST SHENOUDA PRESS
SYDNEY AUSTRALIA 2021

MY HOLY WEEK JOURNAL
COPYRIGHT © 2021
St Shenouda Press

Designed by Caroleen Akladious
artistwork@icloud.com

All rights reserved. Except for brief quotations in critical publications or reviews, no part of this book may be reproduced in any manner without prior written permission from the publisher.

ST SHENOUDA PRESS
8419 Putty Rd,
Putty, NSW 2330
Sydney, Australia

www.stshenoudapress.com

ISBN: 13: 978-0-6451394-2-6

All scripture quotations, unless otherwise indicated, are taken from the New King James Version*. Copyright © 1982 by Thomas Nelson, Inc. Used by permission. All rights reserved.

WHY IS THIS WEEK CALLED PASCHA WEEK?

The word Pascha means "Passover" which is taken from Exodus 12:18 when God said, **"WHEN I SEE THE BLOOD, I WILL PASS OVER YOU"**.

In the first Passover the Israelites were saved by the blood. Our Lord Jesus Christ is referred to as the Passover as it is said, **"FOR INDEED CHRIST, OUR PASSOVER, WAS SACRIFICED FOR US" (1 CORINTHIANS 5:7)**.

Throughout this Holy week we remember the suffering of our Lord Jesus Christ, who offered Himself as a Passover. This happened because, when the Father saw the blood of the Passover, He saved us from the sword of death so as not to perish.

We also remember that His blood was shed for our sake. There is no salvation except through His blood, as it happened at the first Passover (Exodus 12)

PREPARE YOURSELF SPIRITUALLY

It is good during this week, that one sits by himself and remembers his sins, and collects them and puts them at the foot of our Lord's Cross. We put them on the Lamb of God who carried the sins of the whole world.

And says to Him, in shame and pain,
"LORD CARRY MY SINS AS I AM PART OF THE SINS OF THE WHOLE OF MANKIND WHICH YOU CARRIED. TAKE THEM LORD AND NAIL THEM ON THE CROSS WITH YOU AND WIPE THEM WITH YOUR BLOOD."

During Holy Week, examine yourself carefully and diligently. Examine yourself and know that these sins are the cause of His crucifixion.

I am sorry Lord that I made you suffer to that extent. Your suffering is actually my suffering, and You carried them instead of me. Lord I am so grateful with the salvation You have offered to me and to the world with Your blood.

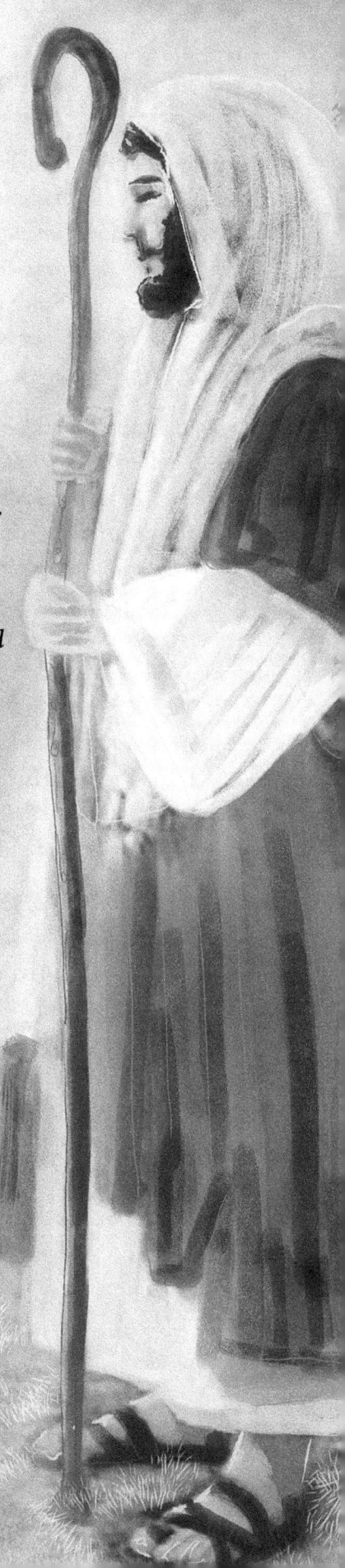

A PRAYER FROM THE DESERT

Lord Jesus Christ, whose will all things obey: pardon what I have done and granted that I, a sinner, may sin no more. Lord, I believe that though I do not deserve it, you can cleanse me from all my sins. Lord, I know that man looks upon the face, but You see the heart. Send Your Spirit into my inmost being, to take possession of my soul and body. Without You I cannot be saved; with You I am protected, I long for Your salvation. And now I ask You for wisdom, deign of Your great goodness to help and defend me. Guide my heart, Almighty God, that I may remember Your presence day and night. Amen.

Holy Week is not a season, but rather a journey. A journey has a purpose. We are going somewhere. We have a destination. And on this journey of Holy Week, we have two specific destinations that we're trying to reach: a CROSS and a TOMB.

"that I may know Him and the power of His resurrection and the fellowship of His sufferings, being conformed to His death."

PHILIPPIANS 3:10

REPENTANCE

Fasting without repentance and changing one's life becomes useless. Unless the fasting person changes his life during fasting, he will only be hungry and exhausted without gaining anything else. Therefore, the Church constantly reminds us of the importance of repentance during fasting. Before Great Lent, we fast Jonah's Fast and we live the story of Jonah and the Ninevites' repentance.

During the third Sunday of Lent, the Holy Church offers us the Gospel reading of the Prodigal Son as a model of repentance, which requires an awakening, confession of sins, leaving the place of sin, and returning to the Heavenly Father with confidence in His mercies and acceptance. This parable reveals to us the depth of God's love for sinners and how He accepts them no matter how horrendous their sin is. Our Lord Jesus Christ said, "the one who comes to Me I will by no means cast out." (John 6:37). Christ "has come to save that which was lost." (Matt 18:11). God desires that all men be saved and come to the knowledge of truth (1 Tim 2:4). Christ is the True Physician who is needed by those who are ill by sin. He did not come to call the righteous, but sinners to repentance (Mark 2:17).

Repentance is a result of divine action; it is the Spirit of God, who moves the hearts of sinners to repent. It is written in the Holy Bible, "For it is God who works in you both to will and do for His good pleasure."(Phil 2:13). God's pleasure is in the return of a sinner so that he will not die in his sin. When God sees His sinful child returning to Him, He has compassion and goes to him, kissing him, and welcomes his return by saying, "It is right that we should make merry and be glad." (Luke 15:32). The return of a sinner and his repentance results in joy to God, as well as all those in heaven, because, "there will be more joy in heaven over one sinner who repents than over ninety-nine just persons who need no repentance." (Luke 15:7).

PRAYERS TO FOCUS ON DURING
HOLY WEEK

PALM SUNDAY
JESUS ENTERS JERUSALEM AS A KING

God prepares His sacrifice. What does this sacrifice mean to you? Among other things, lets pray to begin this journey with Christ with a genuine and firm attitude to make changes in your life.

MONDAY
JESUS CURSES THE FIG TREE AND CLEANSES THE TEMPLE

Jesus cleanses the temple and curses the fig tree. God is preparing those who will accept His sacrifice. Today is a reminder to examine aspects of your life that look like the fig tree. Green from the outside yet has no fruit.

TUESDAY
THE WITHERED FIG TREE AND FURTHER TEACHING

*Jesus teaches in the temple for the last time.
Today is a solemn day, do not go through the motions think of Jesus. The temple leaders publicly challenge and question Jesus, deciding in their hearts to kill Him.*

WEDNESDAY
WOMAN POURS FRAGRANT OIL AND JUDAS BETRAYS JESUS.

A dramatic and deliberate act of repentance takes place. The woman unknowingly prepares Jesus for His burial. Meanwhile, Imagine the intense isolation that Christ felt being the only one to know that Judas will betray Him.

THURSDAY
PASSOVER WASHING OF THE FEET LAST SUPPER – EUCHARIST

Today is an eventful day! Christ washes the feet of His disciples. Christ breaks his body and offers it to His disciples and us. See how Christ loves us. Take and eat. How are you living out Jesus' commandment to wash people's feet and to take and eat?

FRIDAY
TRIAL, CRUCIFIXION 6TH HOUR, DEATH 9TH HOUR, BURIAL 12TH HOUR

Spend time today walking the road to Golgotha with Christ. Read today's Gospel reading, imagining you are there witnessing Jesus' final day and his death. Sit with those emotions, the grief, the emptiness of a world without Christ, the joy of salvation that comes from the cross. Leave it there; nailed to the cross, having faith that Jesus went through these emotions to be with you and to eventually pick you up to glory.

The Holy Week Rite

During this week, the holy Church concentrates on one subject, the Lord Christ's suffering. For this reason, the Psalm readings and the Canonical Hours which cover various subjects relating to the Lord Jesus Christ including His birth, His ministry, His Resurrection, Ascension and sitting on the Father's right hand and His Second Coming in His Glory, are replaced by a special hymn chosen by the Church especially for the Pascha Week in which we address the Lord's suffering for us saying:

"Thine is the Power, the Glory, the Blessing and the Honour, forever Amen, Emmanuel our God and our King"

"Thine is the Power, the Glory, the Blessing and the Honour, forever Amen, Our Lord Jesus Christ my Good Saviour".

"Thine is the Power, the Glory, the Blessing and the Honour, forever Amen ..."

This prayer is repeated ten times every day, five during daytime and five at night, i.e., during the following hours: First, Third, Sixth, Ninth and Eleventh. In each of these prayers, we turn to our God and Saviour in His passions and say, "we know who You are, for "Thine is the Power, Glory, Blessing and Honour, forever Amen."

With this prayer, we follow the Lord Christ step by step along the incidents of this week that preceded the crucifixion.

SPIRITUAL EXERCISES DURING
HOLY WEEK

Things you should be doing during Lent

FIND YOUR MOUNTAIN
This means find a quiet, secret spot where you can be alone to concentrate without any distractions. Don't sit with friends if you'll be tempted to talk. Avoid checking your phone or social media. Spend this week complete focused on Him, talking and listening to Him. Follow His journey to the cross and understand your worth and His love for YOU.

PRAY MORE
Use the times during the readings to contemplate and talk to God.

FOLLOW THE READINGS
Make notes and do the same with the sermons. There's many sermons to listen to instead of listening to music or watching TV.

DO MATANYAS
Do matanyas with the guidance of your confession father

RECITE THE JESUS PRAYER
Try to pray and recite the Jesus Prayer as often as you can. "O my Lord Jesus Christ, have mercy upon me a sinner". You can also add to that prayer, i.e. "O My Lord Jesus Christ, have mercy upon me a sinner and help me to be patient".

"O my Lord JESUS CHRIST HAVE MERCY ON ME a sinner"

PRAYERS TO FOCUS ON DURING
THE HOLY WEEK

Pope Shenouda III

The Holy Week or the Holy Pascha (Passover) is the most important period in the year and the richest spiritually. It is a week full of holy memories of the most crucial stage of salvation and the outstanding chapter in the story of redemption. The church chose for this week certain readings from both the old and the new testaments, which reflect, the most passionate feelings that explain God's relation with Man. The church also chose some deep hymns and spiritual contemplation to suit the occasion.

In the early church, our saintly fathers used to receive this week with respect and reverence, and act in great humility. While fasting, they abstained from eating any sweet food like honey or jam, as they consider it not appropriate to taste any sweet thing while commemorating the lord's suffering for them. Some chose not to cook anything during that week, as a matter of devotion, so that they had more time for worshiping. The majority of Christians used to eat nothing but bread and salt. Those who were physically capable abstained from Friday night till Easter Sunday.

As a sign of devotion during this week, women chose not to put makeup or wear jewellery. People devoted all their time to worshiping; they gathered in churches for prayer and contemplation. The great emperor Theodosius was one of the Christian kings and rulers who ordered all government houses and business to cease work, to enable people to concentrate on worship. Prisoners were also allowed to go to church and join in the ceremonies of this great week, hoping that it would help them to reform. Christian masters also used to relieve their slaves from work all the Pascha week to enable them to worship the Lord like their masters, without any discrimination. So, both masters and slaves were able to worship God and enjoy the effectiveness and depth of this week.

THE PASCHA HYMN

Thine is the Power, the Glory, the Blessing and the Honour, Forever Amen.

We sing this hymn for the Lord Christ throughout Holy Week, following all His movements. We sing it instead of the canonical hours, the five-day prayer and five-night prayers. We repeat the hymn twelve times in each prayer instead of the twelve psalms that are included in each prayer of the canonical hours.

By Pope Shenouda III

The Lord Christ left Jerusalem for Bethany, where we follow Him saying, "Thine is the power, the glory, the blessing and the honour." The chief priests were annoyed when the Lord cleared the temple, and said, "By what authority are you doing these things?" (Mk 11:28) But we say, "Thine is the power, the glory, the blessing, and the honour, Emmanuel our God and King". They planned to kill Him while we defend Him saying, "Thine is the power, the glory, the blessing and the honour, forever amen." The Lord, in humility, bent to wash the disciples' feet, and we praise Him saying "Thine is the power, the glory, the blessing and the honour." The Lord was praying at Gethsemane in such agony that His sweat was like drops of blood and we proclaim Him saying, "Thine is the power and the glory", we follow Him hour by hour; when arrested, put under trial in the presence of His enemies, crowned with thorns, flogged, falling under the cross, nailed, till He commanded His Spirit into the hands of the Father and when He took the robber on His right with Him into paradise, and we sing to Him the hymn, "Thine is the power, the glory, the blessing and the honour, forever. Amen.

The first thing we praise the Lord Jesus Christ for, during the passion week, is His power. Yes, Lord, thine is the power as St. Paul said, "Christ the power of God." (1 Cor 1:24). It is true, Lord that some might think You were weak on the cross, but we know who You are.

The first thing we know about Your power is that you are the creator. "All things were made through Him, and without Him, nothing was made that was made" (Jn 1:3). You have the power of a judge, who will come in glory to judge both the living and the dead. Indeed, this crucified Lord who seemed to the people then weak, had they considered what He had done throughout all the days He spent among them?, they would have known how powerful He had been in everything. He was powerful in His miracles and in His holiness. Lord, You alone of all the powerful, defeated the sin, the world and the devil, while all the others were too weak to resist sin, "For she has cast down many wounded, and all who were slain by her were strong men" (Prov 7:26) as it is written in the Holy Bible, "They have all turned aside, they have together become corrupt; there is none who

does good, no not one" (Ps 14:3). But You God, You are the only one who challenged the whole world, saying, "which of you convicts Me of sin". (Jn 8:46). You are the only one who overcomes the devil and said, "for the ruler of this world is coming, and he has nothing in Me" (Jn 14:30). In the Book of Revelation, they sang for you, "for You alone are holy," (Rev 15:4). You alone are powerful in Your holiness, "holy, harmless, undefiled, separate from sinners, and has become higher than the heavens" (Heb 7:26). Lord, Your miracles proved Your wonderful Power, as You... "had done among them the works which no one else did" (Jn 15:24).

Your power over nature was shown: when You rebuked the wind and the waves and when You walked on the water. David sang for You saying, "You rule the raging of the sea: when its waves rise, You still them" (Ps 89:9). Thine is the Power, O Lord.

You showed Your Power over sickness and death: as You healed all diseases and weaknesses of the people, especially the incurable ones. You opened the eyes of the blind, cleansed those with leprosy, healed the woman suffering from hemorrhages, the 38 years paralytic, the paralyzed who was lowered down through the roof and the man with the withered hand. Lord, You raised the dead, even that who had been in the tomb for four days.

You showed Your Power as a creator: when You fed thousands with five loaves and two fish. You even created a new substance when You turned the water into wine and when You made eyes for the man who was born blind. Your power over the devils was shown by casting away evil spirits, who left many saying, "You are the Son of God." You rebuked the demons and did not let them speak. Your miracles are countless, Lord, as John the Beloved said, "And there are also many other things that Jesus did, which if they were written one by one, I suppose that even the world itself could not contain the books that would be written" (Jn 21:25).

Beside all these aspects of the Lord's Power, the puzzling one is shown in His suffering and crucifixion where He gives us a new concept of the meaning of Power.

WHAT IS THIS NEW CONCEPT OF POWER?

The Lord's new concept of power: the world's concept of power differs from that introduced by the Lord Jesus Christ. To the world, it means violence and the ability to strike, defend oneself and subject others.

By Pope Shenouda III

The Lord set an example of the power which loves and sacrifices, endures, and gives without limits. When we think of power, we have to look at it from a spiritual side, not the physical. That is how we should look at the Lord Christ in His suffering. The materialistic world, poor indeed, thinks that the Lord Christ was weak when they struck Him on the face, mocked Him and crucified Him. That would have been true if the Lord Christ had those insults due to His inability, but in fact, He was far more powerful than all, but He did not because He loved them, and His love was more powerful than death. He was able to put them to death, but He did not because He came to save them from death and by His death to give life.

We glorify the Lord's endurance, which convinces us that, power is in endurance, as the apostle says, "We then who are strong ought to bear with the scruples of the weak, and not to please ourselves" (Rom 15:1). Some people are too weak to endure; even the least insult shows their weakness and lack of power of endurance.

The Lord Christ was powerful in His endurance, and this demonstrates the power of His love. For a person who has love can endure, while failure to endure shows a lack of love.

The Lord Christ came to take away our sins, "all we like sheep have gone astray; we have turned everyone to his way, and the Lord has laid on him the iniquity of us all" (Is 53:6).

The Lord sacrificed himself for our sins and for our sake He endured the insults of those who struck Him and spat on Him. In His deep love, He was joyfully singing in the ear of each of us, "Because for Your sake I have borne reproach; Shame has covered my face" (Ps. 69:7). We listen to these words and answer in humility, "for my sake, you endured the injustice of the evil, the flogging and the slaps, and never turned Your face away from the shameful spitting. The power of the Lord Christ during His passion and crucifixion appear.

In that, He was able to destroy all those who attacked Him, but He never did because of His great love for us. He was punished for our sake and gave us His peace, took upon Himself our shame and gave us His glory.

To understand the real power of the Lord Christ we have to ask ourselves: what could have happened if Christ had refused the humiliation and crucifixion? Or had commanded the earth to swallow all who were on it, or fire to come down from the heavens and burn them?

He could have done so but that would have led to our destruction due to his refusal as a redeemer to die for us. So, the Lord said, "I will die so that you may not die, and be mocked so that you may be glorified. I came especially for your sake to sacrifice myself and endure insults for you out of love for you and for those who insult me". Therefore, He did not only endure injustices but loved, forgave, and prayed for the wicked interceding for them saying, "Father forgive them, for they do not know what they do" (Lk 23:34). This is the real power of a heart full of love, who tolerates those who trespass against Him, loves them, prays for them and sacrificed Himself for their sake.

Who of us can follow the same example and when insulted by another inferior to his rank, would forgive, defend and also promote him! St. Peter, the Apostle, drew his sword to defend his mater when they arrested him and he cut off the slave's ear not understanding power in its Christian spiritual concept, so the Lord asked him to put his sword back. It is good to have holy zeal, but violence is not our way. Our way is love. With this love, the Lord healed his ear and surrendered to the sinners for whose redemption He came. St John and St James the apostles also did not understand the real meaning of power and when the Lord Christ was rejected by a city, the two disciples said, "Lord, do You want us to command fire to come down from heaven and consume them, just as Elijah did?" But He turned and rebuked them, and said, "You do not know what manner of spirit you are of. For the Son of Man did not come to destroy men's lives but to save them." (Lk 9:54-56).

In the same way, the Lord came willfully to the cross, to give His life a ransom for many. When we stand near the cross, we do not weep as did Mary Magdalene and the daughter of Jerusalem… not do we pity the Lord nor blame Him, we stand near the cross to glorify both the cross and the crucified, singing the beautiful hymn. Thine is the Power.

Morning
PALM SUNDAY
OF HOLY WEEK

9TH HOUR

Out of the mouth of babes and infants You have ordained strength, Because of Your enemies, That You may silence the enemy and the avenger. When I consider Your heavens, the work of Your fingers, The moon and the stars, which You have ordained. Alleluia (Psalm 8:2-3)

Morning
PALM SUNDAY
OF HOLY WEEK

11TH HOUR

Out of the mouth of babes and infants you have ordained strength, O Lord our Lord, how excellent is, Your name in all the earth. Alleluia. (Psalm 8:2)

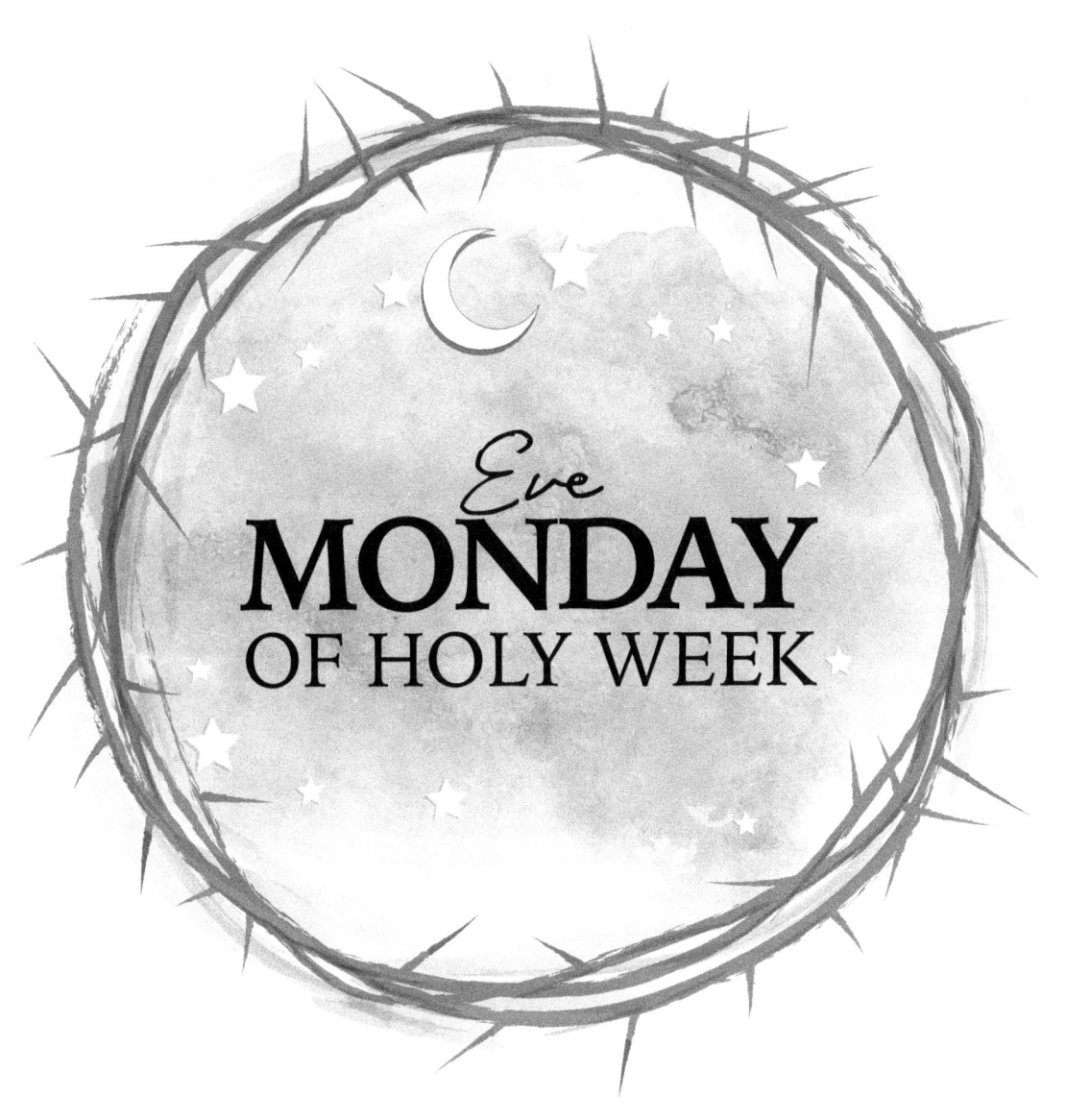

Eve MONDAY OF HOLY WEEK

1ST HOUR

I will sing praises to the Lord. Hear, O Lord, when I cry with my voice! Have mercy also upon me, and answer me. When You said, "Seek My face," My heart said to You, "Your face, Lord I will seek. Alleluia (Psalm 27:6-8)

Eve MONDAY OF HOLY WEEK

3RD HOUR

Save Your people, And bless Your inheritance; Shepherd them also, And bear them up forever. Hear the voice of my supplications When I cry to You, When I lift up my hands toward Your holy sanctuary. Alleluia. (Psalm 28:9)

Eve MONDAY OF HOLY WEEK

6TH HOUR

Give unto the Lord, O you mighty ones, Give unto the Lord glory and strength. Give unto the Lord the glory due to His name; Worship the Lord in the beauty of holiness. Alleluia (Psalm 29: 1-2)

Eve MONDAY OF HOLY WEEK

I have called upon You, for You will hear me, O God; Incline Your ear to me, and hear my speech. Hear a just cause, Lord, Attend to my cry. Alleluia (Psalm 17:6)

Eve MONDAY OF HOLY WEEK

11TH HOUR

He delivered me from my strong enemy, From those who hated me, For they were too strong for me. They confronted me in the day of my calamity. But the Lord was my support. Alleluia. (Psalm 18:17-18)

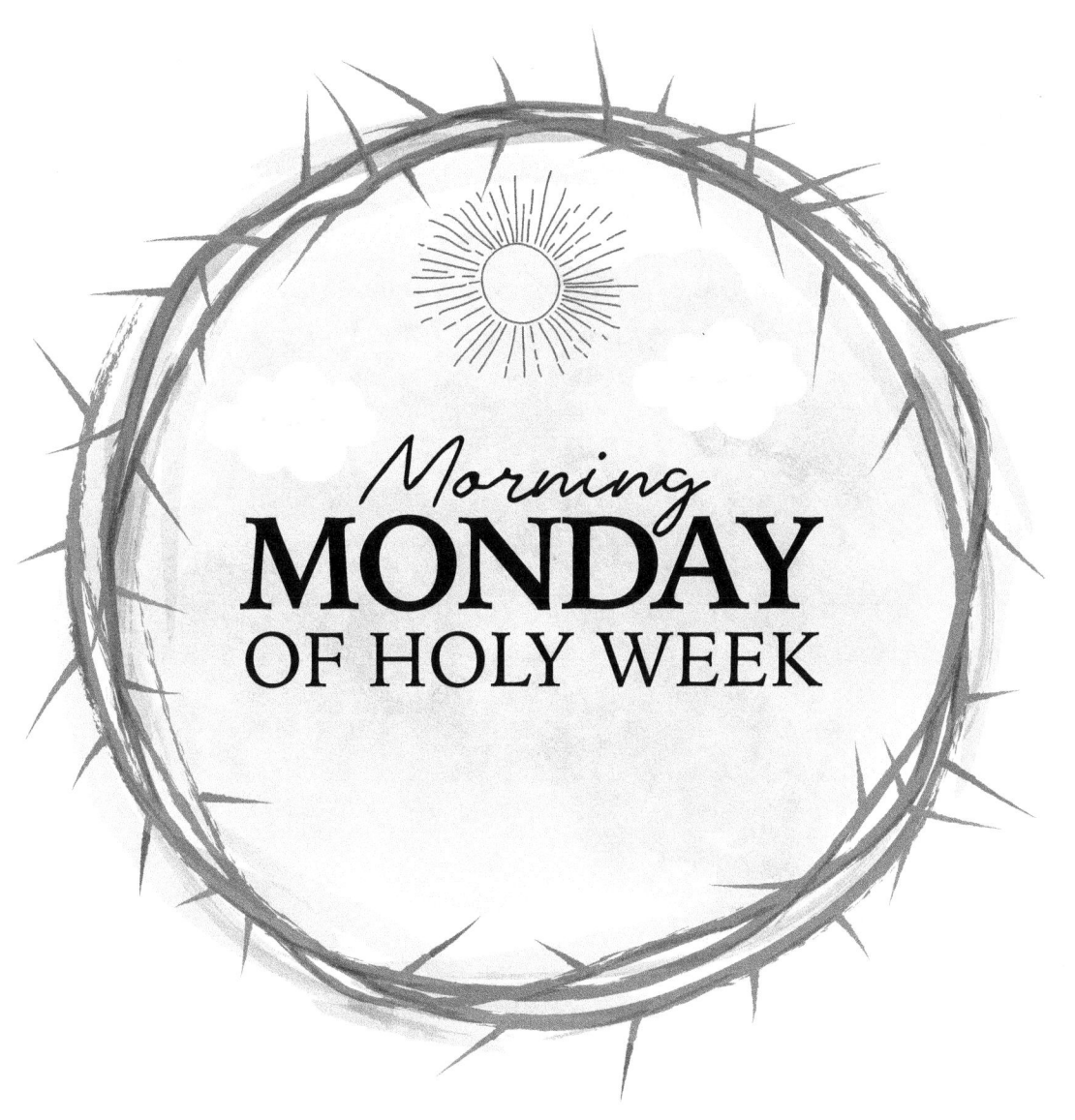

Morning MONDAY OF HOLY WEEK

Blessed be the Lord God, the God of Israel, Who only does wondrous things!, And blessed be His glorious name forever! And let the whole earth be filled with His glory. Amen and Amen. (Psalm 72:18-19)

Morning MONDAY OF HOLY WEEK

I was glad when they said to me, "Let us go into the house of the Lord." Our feet have been standing Within your gates, O Jerusalem! Alleluia. (Psalm 122:1-2)

Morning
MONDAY
OF HOLY WEEK

6TH HOUR

Where the tribes go up, The tribes of the Lord, To the Testimony of Israel, To give thanks to the name of the Lord. Alleluia. (Psalm 122:4)

Morning
MONDAY
OF HOLY WEEK

9TH HOUR

You will answer us, O God of our salvation, You who are the confidence of all the ends of the earth, And of the far off seas; Blessed is the man whom You choose, And cause to approach You, That he may dwell in Your courts. Alleluia (Psalm 65:5)

Morning
MONDAY
OF HOLY WEEK

11TH HOUR

Consider and hear me, O Lord my God; Enlighten my eyes, Lest I sleep the sleep of death; Lest my enemy say, "I have prevailed against him". Alleluia. (Psalm 13:3-4)

Eve
TUESDAY
OF HOLY WEEK

1ST HOUR

In God is my salvation and my glory; The rock of my strength, And my refuge, is in God. He only is my rock and my salvation; He is my defense; I shall not be greatly moved. Alleluia. (Psalm 62:7, 62:2)

Eve TUESDAY OF HOLY WEEK

3RD HOUR

Consider and hear me, O Lord my God; Enlighten my eyes, Lest I sleep the sleep of death; But I have trusted in Your mercy; My heart shall rejoice in Your salvation. Alleluia (Psalm 13:3, 5)

Eve TUESDAY OF HOLY WEEK

6TH HOUR

I will say of the Lord, "He is my refuge and my fortress; My God, in Him I will trust." Surely He shall deliver you from the snare of the fowler And from the perilous pestilence. Alleluia. (Psalm 91:2-3)

Eve TUESDAY
OF HOLY WEEK

9TH HOUR

The Lord brings the counsel of the nations to nothing; He makes the plans of the peoples of no effect. The counsel of the Lord stands forever, The plans of His heart to all generations. Alleluia. (Psalm 33:10-11)

Eve
TUESDAY
OF HOLY WEEK

11TH HOUR

Where the tribes go up, The tribes of the Lord, To the Testimony of Israel, To give thanks to the name of the Lord. Alleluia. (Psalm 122:4)

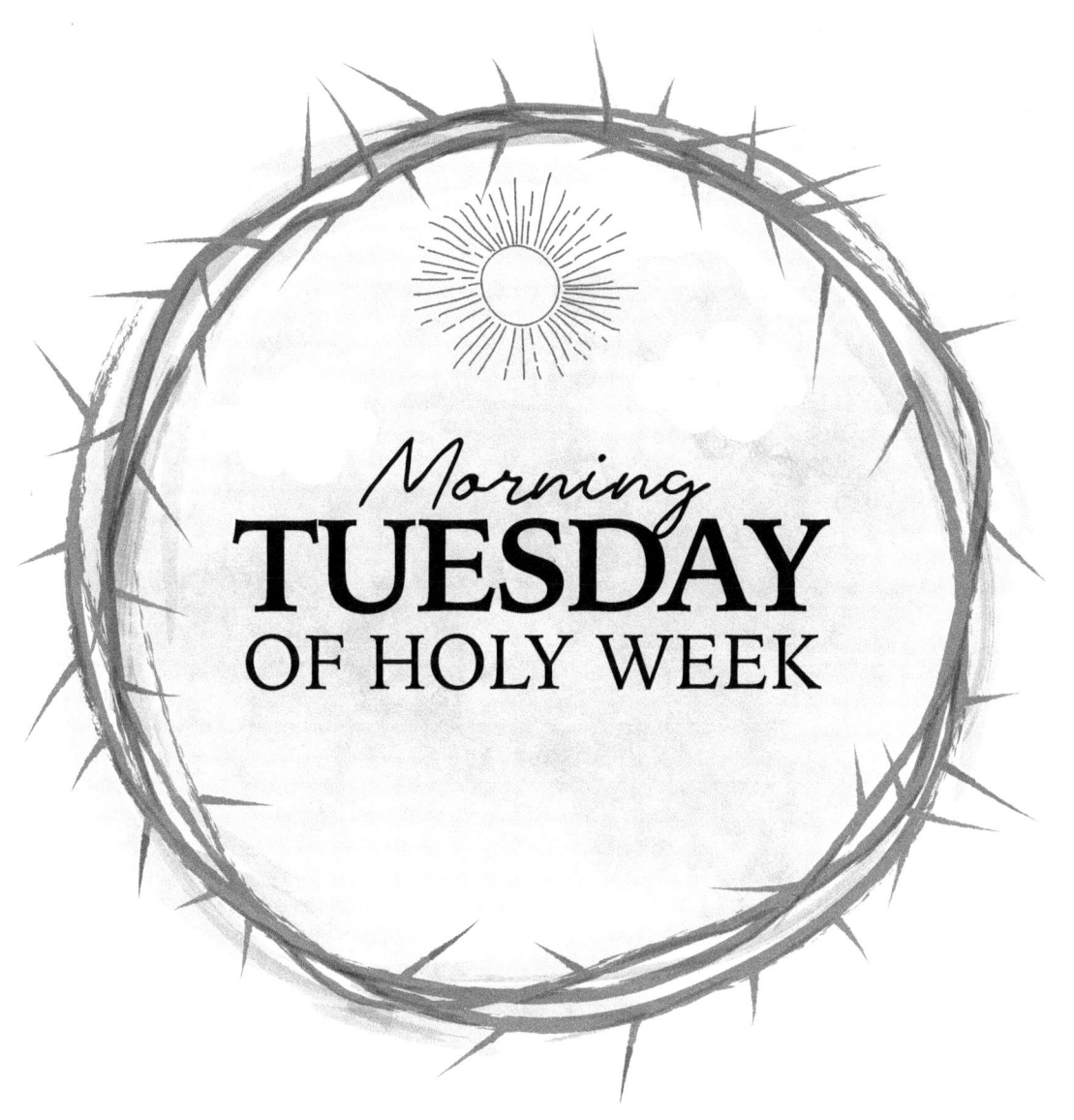

Morning
TUESDAY
OF HOLY WEEK

1ST HOUR

Deliver my soul, O Lord, from lying lips And from a deceitful tongue. My soul has dwelt too long with one who hates peace. I am for peace; But when I speak, they are for war. Alleluia (Psalm 120:2, 6-7)

Morning TUESDAY OF HOLY WEEK

Plead my cause and redeem me; Revive me according to Your word. Salvation is far from the wicked, For they do not seek Your statutes. Alleluia. (Psalm 119:154-155)

Morning
TUESDAY
OF HOLY WEEK

6TH HOUR

He delivers me from my enemies. You also lift me up above those who rise against me; You have delivered me from the violent man. He delivered me from my strong enemy, From those who hated me, For they were too strong for me. Alleluia (Psalm 18:48, 17)

Morning
TUESDAY
OF HOLY WEEK

To You, O Lord, I lift my soul. O my God, I trust in You; Let me not be ashamed; Let not my enemies triumph over me. Indeed, Let those be ashamed who deal treacherously without cause. Alleluia (Psalm 25:1-3)

Morning TUESDAY OF HOLY WEEK

Your Throne, O God, is forever and ever; A sceptre of righteousness is the sceptre of Your kingdom. Blessed is he who considers the poor; The Lord deliver him in time of trouble. Alleluia (Psalms 45:6, 41:1)

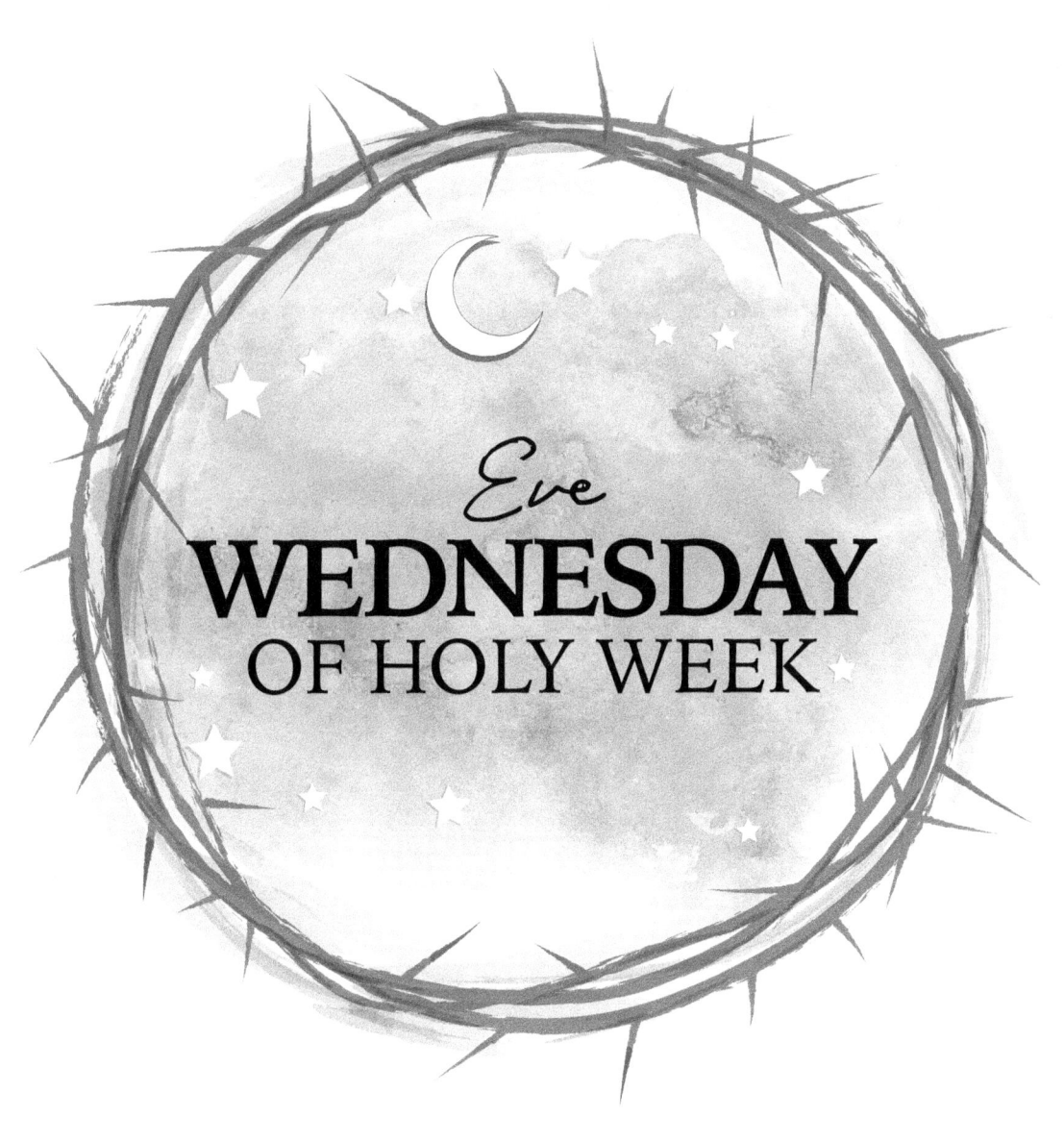

Eve
WEDNESDAY
OF HOLY WEEK

1ST HOUR

You have been my defence And refuge in the day of my trouble. To You, O my Strength, I will sing praises; For God is my defence, My God of mercy. Alleluia. (Psalm 59:16-17)

Eve
WEDNESDAY
OF HOLY WEEK

3RD HOUR

Blessed is the man whom You choose, And cause to approach You, That he may dwell in Your courts. Holy is Your temple. Awesome in righteousness. Alleluia (Psalm 65:4-5)

Eve WEDNESDAY OF HOLY WEEK

6TH HOUR

Hear my prayer, O Lord, And let my cry come to You. In the day that I call, answer me speedily. Alleluia (Psalm 102:1-2)

Eve WEDNESDAY OF HOLY WEEK

9TH HOUR

Deliver Me from the sword, My precious life from the power of the dog. Save Me from the lion's mouth And from the horns of the wild oxen! You have answered Me. Alleluia. (Psalm 22:20-21)

Eve
WEDNESDAY
OF HOLY WEEK

11TH HOUR

Be merciful to me, O God, be merciful to me! For my soul trusts in You; And in the shadow of Your wings I will make my refuge, Until these calamities have passed by. Alleluia (Psalm 57:1)

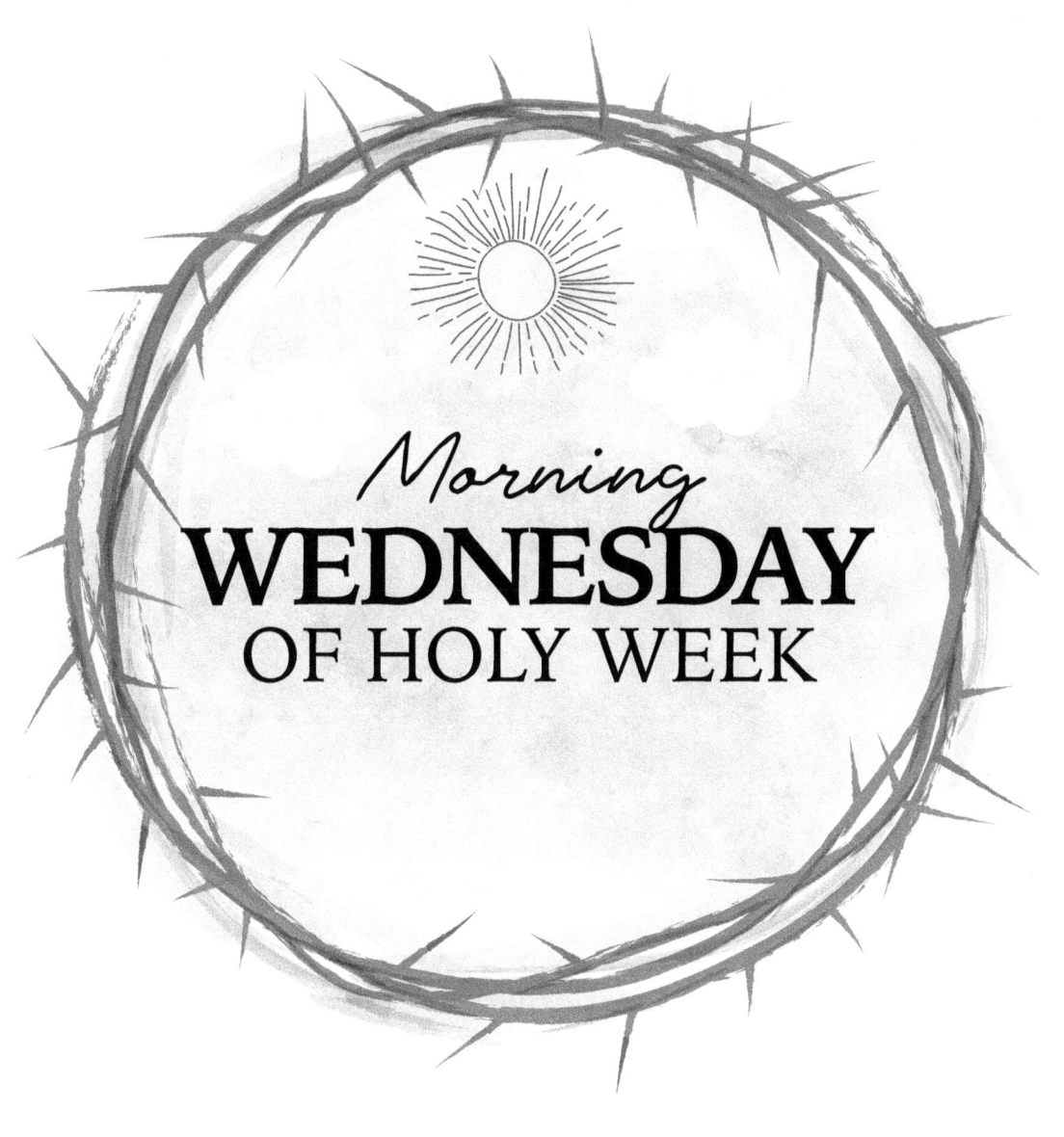

Morning
WEDNESDAY
OF HOLY WEEK

1ST HOUR

That You may be found just when You speak, And blameless when You judge. The Lord brings the counsel of the nations to nothing; He makes the plans of the peoples of no effect. Alleluia. (Psalms 51:4, 33:10)

Morning
WEDNESDAY
OF HOLY WEEK

3RD HOUR

And if he comes to see me, he speaks lies; His heart gathers iniquity to itself; When he goes out, he tells it. Blessed is he who considers the poor; The Lord will deliver him in time of trouble. Alleluia. (Psalm 41:6, 1)

Morning
WEDNESDAY
OF HOLY WEEK

6TH HOUR

For behold, Your enemies make a tumult; And those who hate You have lifted up their head. For they have consulted together with one consent; They form a confederacy against You.: Alleluia. (Psalm 83:2, 5)

Morning
WEDNESDAY
OF HOLY WEEK

9TH HOUR

My enemies speak evil of me: "When will he die, and his name perish?" And if he comes to see me, he speaks lies; His heart gathers iniquity to itself. Alleluia (Psalm 41:5-6)

Morning
WEDNESDAY
OF HOLY WEEK

O Lord, heal me, for my bones are troubled. My soul also is greatly troubled. And do not hide Your face from Your servant, For I am in trouble; Hear me speedily. Alleluia. (Psalms 6:2-3, 69:17)

Eve THURSDAY
OF HOLY WEEK

Eve THURSDAY OF HOLY WEEK

1ST HOUR

Save me, O God! For the waters have come up to my neck. O God, in the multitude of Your mercy, Hear me in the truth of Your salvation. Alleluia (Psalm 69:1, 13)

Eve
THURSDAY
OF HOLY WEEK

3RD HOUR

His words were softer than oil, Yet they were drawn swords. Give ear to my prayer, O God, And do not hide Yourself from my supplication. Alleluia (Psalm 55:21, 1)

Eve
THURSDAY
OF HOLY WEEK

Deliver me, O Lord, from evil men; Preserve me from violent men, Who plan evil things in their hearts; They continually gather together for war. Alleluia. (Psalm 140:1-2)

Eve THURSDAY OF HOLY WEEK

O Lord my God, in You I put my trust; Save me from all those who persecute me; And deliver me, Lest they tear me like a lion. Alleluia. (Psalm 7:1-2)

Eve THURSDAY OF HOLY WEEK

11TH HOUR

In God is my salvation and my glory; The rock of my strength, And my refuge, is in God. He only is my rock and my salvation; He is my defence; I shall not be greatly moved. Alleluia. (Psalm 62:7, 2)

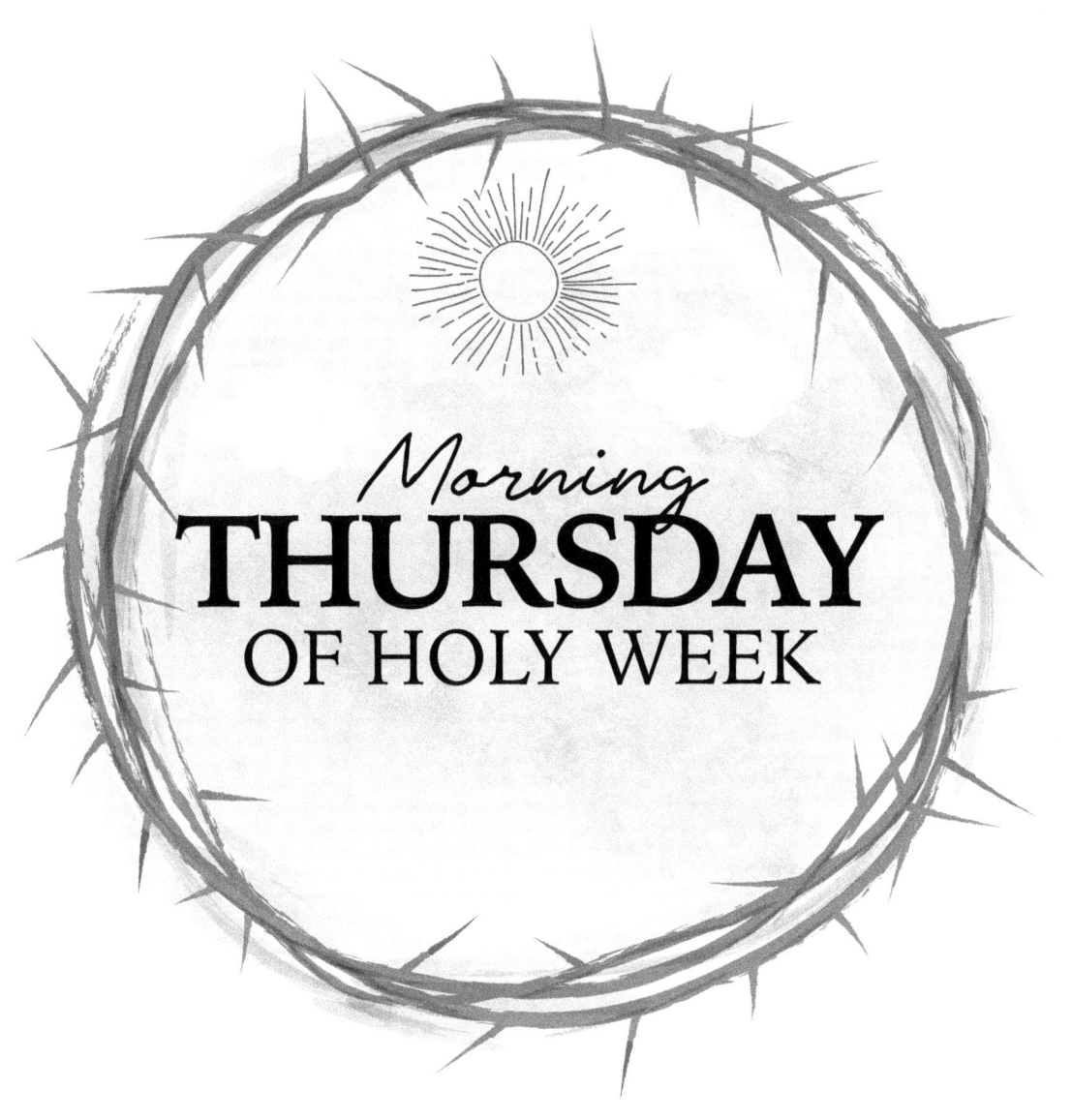

Morning
THURSDAY
OF HOLY WEEK

1ST HOUR

The words of his mouth were smoother than butter, But war was in his heart; His words were softer than oil, Yet they were drawn swords. For it is not an enemy who reproaches me; Then I could bear it. Nor is it one who hates me who has magnified himself against me; Then I could hide from him. Alleluia (Psalm 55:21, 12)

Morning
THURSDAY
OF HOLY WEEK

They gather together against the life of the righteous, and condemn innocent blood. He has brought on them their own iniquity and wickedness. The Lord our God shall cut them off. Alleluia. (Psalm 94:21, 23)

Morning
THURSDAY
OF HOLY WEEK

6TH HOUR

Let the lying lips be put to silence, Which speak insolent things proudly and contemptuously against the righteous. For I hear the slander of many; Fear is on every side; While they take counsel together against me, They scheme to take away my life. Alleluia. (Psalm 31:18, 13)

Morning
THURSDAY
OF HOLY WEEK

9TH HOUR

The Lord is my shepherd; I shall not want. He makes me to lie down in green pastures; He leads me beside the still waters. Alleluia (Psalm 23:1-2)

Morning
THURSDAY
OF HOLY WEEK

11TH HOUR

Seeing you hate instruction And cast My words behind you? When you saw a thief, you consented with him, And have been a partaker with adulterers. Alleluia. (Psalm 50:17-18)

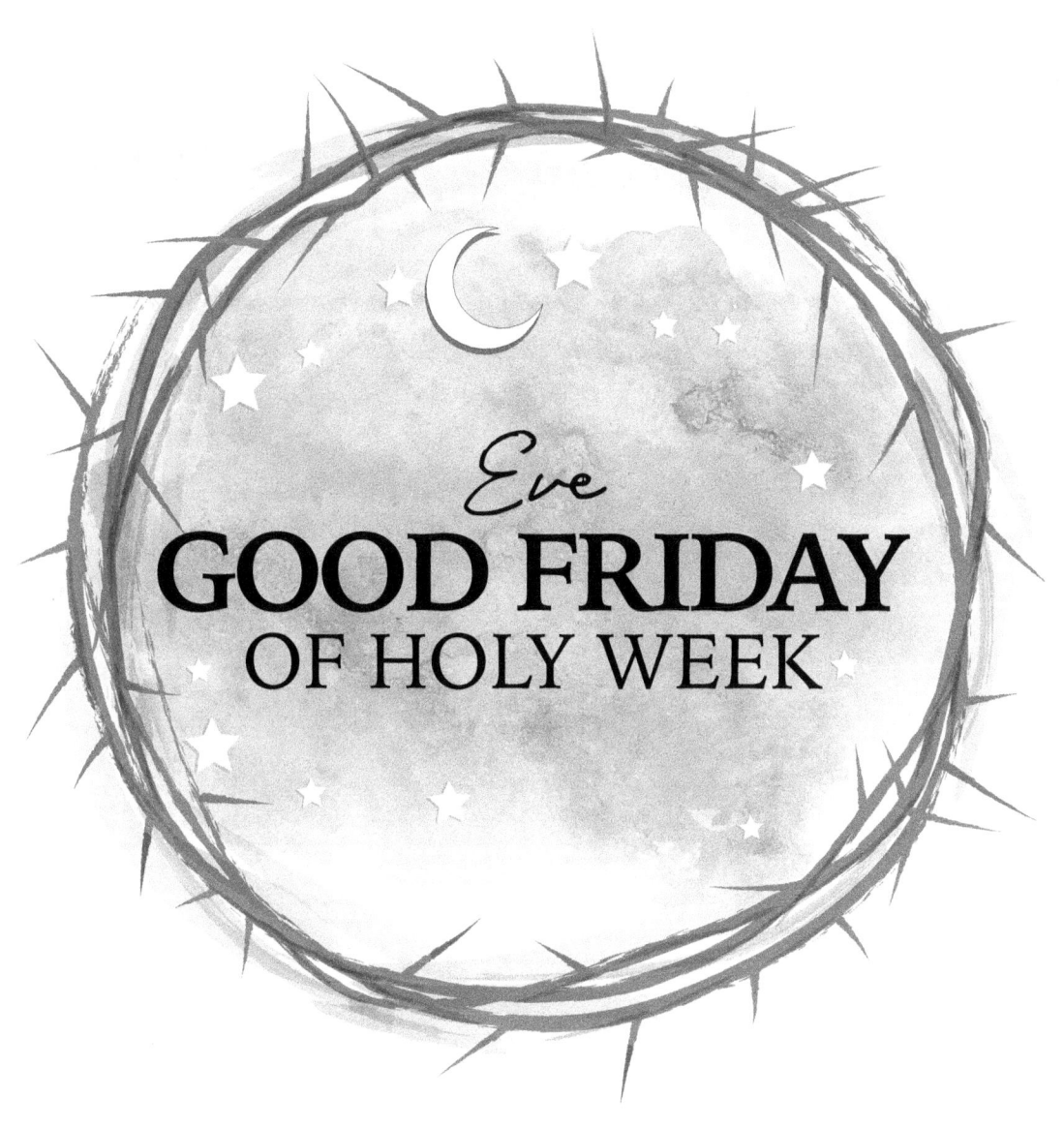

Eve GOOD FRIDAY OF HOLY WEEK

1ST HOUR

Hear my prayer, O Lord, And let my cry come to You. My enemies reproach me all day long, Those who deride me swear an oath against me. Alleluia (Psalm 102:1, 8)

Eve
GOOD FRIDAY
OF HOLY WEEK

3RD HOUR

Do not keep silent, O God of my praise! For the mouth of the wicked and the mouth of the deceitful Have opened against me; They have also surrounded me with words of hatred, And fought against me without a cause. Alleluia (Psalm 109:1-3)

Eve
GOOD FRIDAY
OF HOLY WEEK

6TH HOUR

Deliver me from my enemies, O my God: Defend me from those who rise up against me. I looked for someone to take pity, but there was none; And for comforters, but I found none. Alleluia (Psalm 59:1, 69:20)

Eve
GOOD FRIDAY
OF HOLY WEEK

9TH HOUR

Who speak peace to their neighbours, But evil is in their hearts. Give them according to their deeds, And according to the wickedness of their endeavours. Let those be put to shame and brought to dishonour Who seek after my life; Let those be turned back and brought to confusion Who plot my hurt. Alleluia (Psalms 28:3-4, 35:4)

Eve
GOOD FRIDAY
OF HOLY WEEK

11TH HOUR

Why do the nations rage, and the people plot a vain thing? The kings of the earth set themselves, And the rulers take council together, Against the Lord and against His Anointed. He who sits in the heavens shall laugh; The Lord shall hold them in derision. Then He shall speak to them in His wrath, And distress them in His deep displeasure. (Psalm 2:1-5)

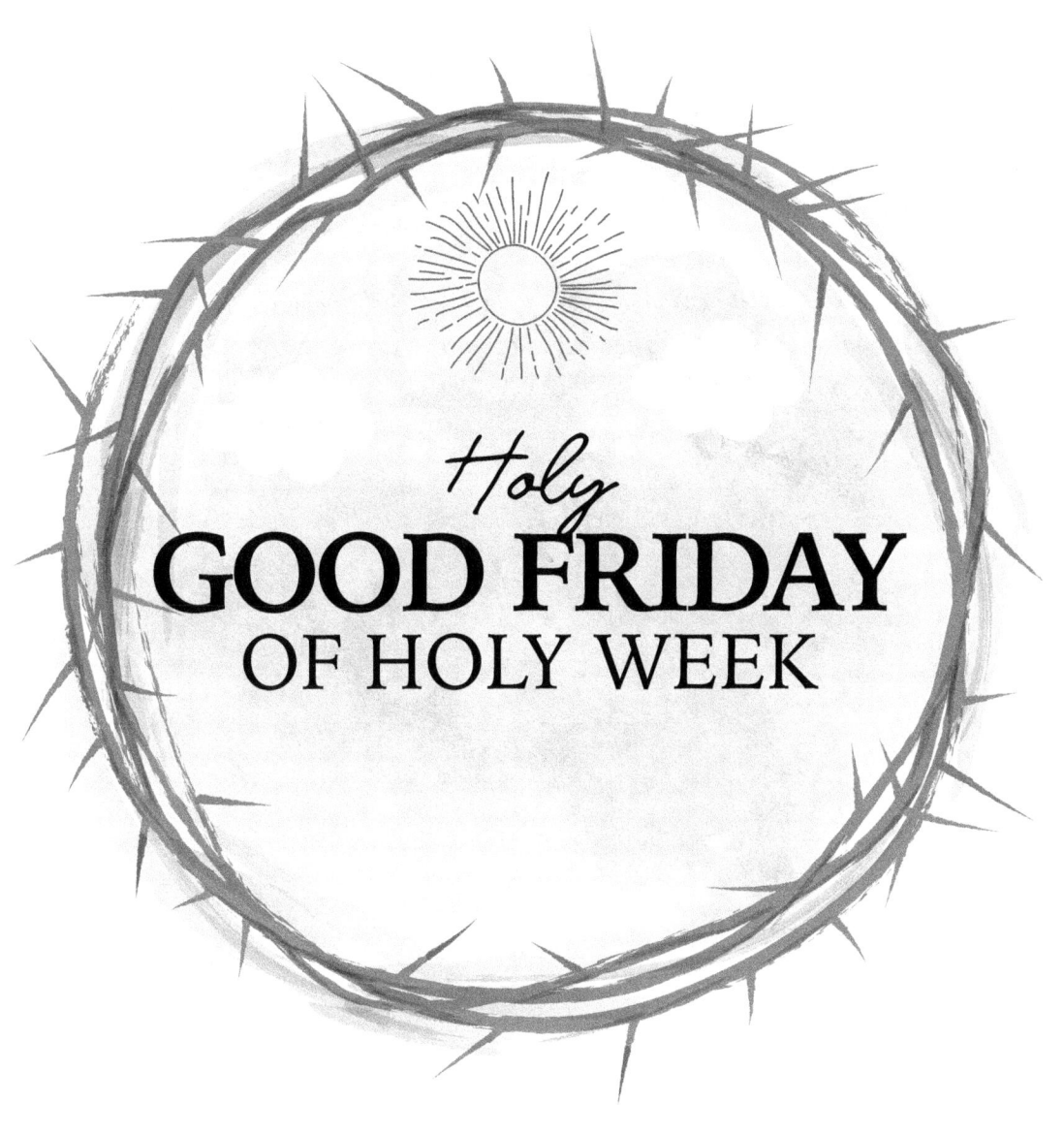

Holy GOOD FRIDAY
OF HOLY WEEK

1st HOUR

For false witnesses have risen against me and injustice has deceived itself, fierce witnesses rise up,; They ask me things that I do not know, They reward me evil for good, They gnashed at me with their teeth. Alleluia. (Psalms 27:12, 35:11-12, 16)

Holy GOOD FRIDAY
OF HOLY WEEK

3RD HOUR

For I am ready to fall, And my sorrow is continually before me. For dogs have surrounded Me. The congregation of the wicked has enclosed Me. Alleluia. (Psalms 38:17, 22:16)

Holy
GOOD FRIDAY
OF HOLY WEEK

6TH HOUR

They did not accept Me, I who is love, but refused me as a dead body, they drove nails into my body and therefore do not forsake Me, O Lord; and God. `They pierced My hands and My feet and counted all My bones. They divide My garments among them, And for My clothing they cast lots. They shoot out the lip, they shake the head, saying, "He trusted in the Lord, let Him rescue Him; Let Him deliver Him, since He delights in Him. Alleluia (Psalms 38:21-22, 22:16-18, 7-8)

Holy GOOD FRIDAY OF HOLY WEEK

9TH HOUR

Save me, O God! For the waters have come up to my neck. I sink in deep mire, Where there is no standing; I have come into deep waters, Where the floods overflow me. They also gave me gall for my food, And for my thirst they gave me vinegar to drink. Alleluia.
(Psalm 69:1-2, 21)

Holy
GOOD FRIDAY
OF HOLY WEEK

11TH HOUR

I spread out my hands to You so answer me speedily O Lord for my spirit fails, do not hide Your face from me lest I be like those who go down into the pit. Into Your hand I commit my spirit; You have redeemed me, O Lord God of truth. Alleluia (Psalms 144:6-7, 31:5)

Holy
GOOD FRIDAY
OF HOLY WEEK

12TH HOUR

You have laid me in the lowest pit and in dark places and the shadow of death, Yea though I walk through the valley of the shadow of death, I will fear no evil; For you are with me. Your throne, O God, is forever and ever; A sceptre of righteousness is the sceptre of Your kingdom. All Your garments are scented with myrrh and aloes and cassia, Out of the ivory places, by which they have made You glad. Alleluia (Psalms 88:6, 23:4)

Bright SATURDAY OF HOLY WEEK

MATINS

I am like a man who has no strength, Adrift among the dead, Awake! Why do You sleep, O Lord? Arise! Do not cast us off forever. Arise for our help, And redeem us for Your mercies sake. Then our mouth was filled with laughter, And our tongue with singing. Then they said among the nations, "The Lord has done great things for them." The Lord has done great things for us. Whereof we are glad. Alleluia. (Psalms 88:4-5, 44:23, 26, 126:2-3)

Bright SATURDAY OF HOLY WEEK

3RD HOUR

For You will not leave my soul in Sheol, Nor will You allow Your Holy One to see corruption. You will show me the path of life; In Your presence is fullness of joy. Alleluia (Psalm 16:10-11)

Bright
SATURDAY
OF HOLY WEEK

Out of the depths I have cried to You, O Lord; Bring my soul out of prison, That I may praise Your name, O Lord. Alleluia. (Psalms 130:1, 142:7)

Bright
SATURDAY
OF HOLY WEEK

9TH HOUR

But you, O Lord be merciful to me, and raise me up, that I may repay them. My enemies speak evil of me; "When will he die, and his name perish?" Alleluia (Psalm 41:10, 41:5)

Joyous
SATURDAY
LITURGY

I lay down and slept; I awoke, for the Lord sustained me. But You, O Lord, are a shield for me. My glory and the one who lifts up my head. Arise, O God, judge the earth; For You shall inherit all nations. Alleluia (Psalms 3:5, 82:8)

Joyous SATURDAY LITURGY

Let God arise, Let His enemies be scattered; Let those who hate Him flee before Him. Alleluia (Psalm 68:1)

Joyous EASTER RESURRECTION

Then the Lord awoke as one out of sleep, And like a mighty man who shouts because of wine. And He built His sanctuary like the heights, Like the earth which He has established forever. Alleluia. (Psalm 78:65, 69)

Joyous EASTER RESURRECTION

This is the day which the Lord has made; We will rejoice and be glad in it. Save us, O Lord and ease our ways. Lord God has given us Light. Alleluia. (Psalm 118:24-25, 27)

THE PROCESSION OF THE RESURRECTION ICON

Fr Bishoy Kamel

During the liturgy of the Resurrection Feast and during the liturgies of the Holy fifty days, the Priests and Deacons go around the church three times in their royal garments offering incense before the icon of the Resurrection, while the whole congregation joyously and triumphantly sing: "Christ is risen from the dead. With His death He crushed death. He gave those who were dead eternal life"

THIS IS A PROCESSION OF THREE LIVING ICONS
PARTICIPATING WITH CHRIST'S RESURRECTION

FIRST ICON

This icon is the one before which the Priest offers incense. This icon is anointed with Holy oil radiating the live-giving spirit of the Resurrection and filling the whole church with power and great glory.

SECOND ICON

This icon is traditional in that the baptism of the catechumens (their burial followed by their resurrection in baptism) took place on the night of the Feast of the Resurrection. The Church then paraded them in the icon's procession, thus becoming the Second Icon on the night of the Feast of the Resurrection having been raised with Christ from the dead. What a magnificent icon! The Church lives in the Resurrection.

THIRD ICON

This icon is the most magnificent of all the icons. It is the Church who lives the power of the Resurrection with Christ through a life of repentance and death to the world. Each soul in church sings loudly "Christ rose us with Him. He broke the thorn of death and gave us life".

How beautiful is the Church whose whole congregation leads a life of repentance with the Resurrected Christ? This is a congregation which is a living icon of the Resurrected Christ.

This is the living procession of the Resurrection, during which we sing the triumphing hymn of salvation. This is also the hymn of our death to the world:

"Christ is risen and raised us up with Him. He crushed death by His own death. He blessed us with eternal life, we who were dead in the tombs of sin."

My friends, during the Resurrection Prayers let us make our lives a true icon of the Resurrected Christ. Let us make all the days of our life holy and joyous.

www.ingramcontent.com/pod-product-compliance
Lightning Source LLC
La Vergne TN
LVHW081355060426
835510LV00013B/1835